Eating and living

This section explains what happens to food inside your body and provides some useful tips on good and bad diet habits.

Growing up

In this section, you can find out what happens when you start to develop an adult's body during your teenage years.

Skin, hair, teeth and nails

In this section you can find out about the parts you can see on the outside of your body – your skin, hair, teeth and nails.

Pregnancy and birth

Fully grown adult bodies can produce babies. This section tells you what happens during lovemaking, pregnancy and birth.

Caring for your body

If you care properly for your body, you will help yourself to stay healthy. You can do this by exercising regularly and avoiding addictive substances such as tobacco, drugs and excessive alcohol. In this section you can find out why these things are harmful, and there are some important tips on exercising to keep in trim.

A guide to the body

What are you made of?

Your body is built from millions and millions of microscopic building blocks called cells. There are dozens of different kinds of cells, each type designed to do a specific job within the body.

Cells don't work alone. They join together to form organs: large groups of cells bound together to do a particular job. Your heart and lungs are examples of organs.

All about cells

There are many different types of body cells. They are all so tiny that you can only see them under a microscope. A few examples of different cell shapes are shown on the right.

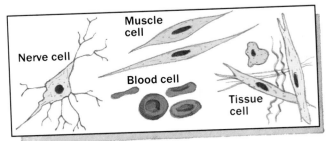

Muscle cell

Nerve cell

Blood cell

Tissue cell

Cell division leads to growth.

Cells can make copies of themselves by dividing in two. Some cells can even change from one sort into another. As your cells divide and change, you grow.

Waste products

Food and oxygen

All your cells must be provided with oxygen and food in order to survive and work. They produce waste materials as they work, including carbon dioxide gas.

What's in your body?

The main parts of the body are introduced below. You can find out more about them all in this book.

SKIN stops you drying out and protects your internal organs. It is covered in fine hairs which help to protect it and keep it warm.

Your EYES, NOSE, MOUTH and EARS gather information and send it to your brain in the form of tiny electrical signals.

Your SKELETON has 206 different bones which support the body and protect its soft parts. Bones are full of nerves and blood vessels.

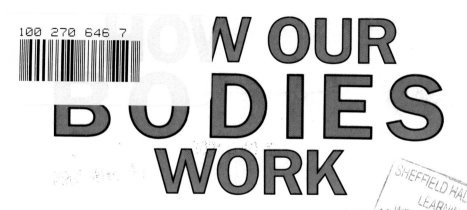

W OUR BODIES WORK

Written by

Nick Davies

Edited by

Moira Butterfield

Illustrated by

Shelagh McNicholas, Merida Woodford and Guy Smith

Designed by

Mike Pringle, Brian Robertson and Teresa Foster

CONTENTS

BBC

About this book

Your body is a very complex piece of machinery. It has lots of different parts which work together to keep you alive. In this book, you can find out how it functions and how to look after it. After all, it's the only one you'll get!

When you become a teenager, you develop physically. This process can be worrying, but you are likely to feel happier if you understand what is happening. In this book there are explanations of the changes you will experience.

How to use this book

This book is split up into separate sections. In each section you can find out how a specific part of your body works. There are nine different sections in all.

Guide to the body
These two pages provide an introduction to the most important systems and parts to be found in the human body.

Body movement
Without your bones and muscles, you couldn't move. These clever but simple body parts are explained in this section.

Sensing the world
Your senses are hearing, sight, smell, taste and touch. This section is about how they work and how the brain controls them.

Your heart and lungs
Blood is pumped around by your heart and supplied with oxygen by your lungs. This section explains the system.

MUSCLES allow the body to move and bend. They run from one bone to another and are joined to each bone by tough fibres called tendons. The muscles shorten or lengthen (contract or relax) in order to move bones together or apart.

The NERVOUS SYSTEM is made up of nerves connected to the brain. The nerves carry messages in the form of electrical signals to and from the brain and all the body parts. The brain processes the information rather like a computer.

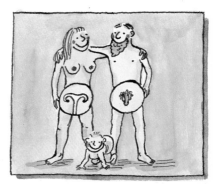

BLOOD is the body's transport system. It takes food and oxygen to all the body cells and carries waste away from them. The heart constantly pumps the blood around.

The LUNGS are two sponge-like bags in the rib-cage. When you breathe in, you suck air into them and oxygen passes into your blood through the lung walls. When you breathe out, you get rid of waste carbon dioxide made by your body.

The REPRODUCTIVE SYSTEM is made up of body parts which can produce a baby. In women, the ovaries make eggs that can grow into babies. In men, the testes make sperm which come out via the penis and can join with an egg when a man and a woman make love.

The DIGESTIVE SYSTEM is made up of the stomach, intestines and liver. Food is broken up by digestive juices in the stomach and the intestines.

Tiny parts called NUTRIENTS are absorbed through the intestines into the blood, which carries them to the liver. The liver stores them and sends them to the body cells

The EXCRETORY SYSTEM is made up of the kidneys, bladder and bowels. The kidneys clean blood and make urine, which is stored in the bladder until it leaves the body.

Sensing the world

Millions of sensitive 'receptor' cells all over your body constantly send tiny signals to your brain.

Your brain sends messages back all the time. Your nervous system relays all the information.

Messages to and fro

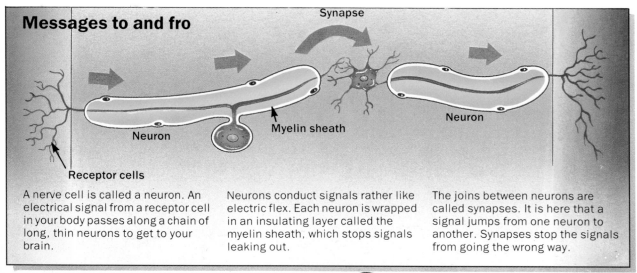

A nerve cell is called a neuron. An electrical signal from a receptor cell in your body passes along a chain of long, thin neurons to get to your brain.

Neurons conduct signals rather like electric flex. Each neuron is wrapped in an insulating layer called the myelin sheath, which stops signals leaking out.

The joins between neurons are called synapses. It is here that a signal jumps from one neuron to another. Synapses stop the signals from going the wrong way.

The wiring system

The neuron chains in your body are bundled together en route to and from the brain. They form a network of fine cables called nerves.

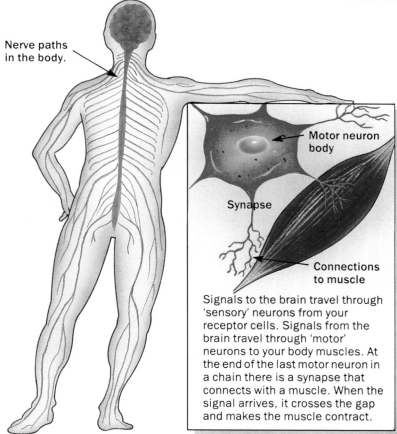

Signals to the brain travel through 'sensory' neurons from your receptor cells. Signals from the brain travel through 'motor' neurons to your body muscles. At the end of the last motor neuron in a chain there is a synapse that connects with a muscle. When the signal arrives, it crosses the gap and makes the muscle contract.

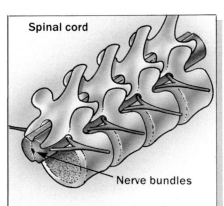

Signals to and from the brain travel via the spinal cord, a bony tube that goes up your back. Lots of nerve cells are bundled together up the middle of the cord. They come in or out through small holes and gaps between the bones.

The human telephone exchange

The brain and the spinal cord work rather like a telephone exchange, receiving and sending out messages all the time. They are called the 'Central Nervous System' (CNS for short).

Your motor neurons, sensory neurons and receptor cells are called the 'Peripheral Nervous System' (PNS for short). Every part of your body has its own bit of PNS.

Some parts of your PNS carry messages to and from your internal organs. You have no conscious control over these organs, and don't feel them working, so this part of your nervous system is called the Autonomic Nervous System (ANS for short). It does all the boring jobs for you, such as making sure you breathe when you're asleep!

Emergency messages

Electrical signals travel through your nervous system fast enough to cover the length of a football pitch in one second! So messages get to your brain quickly.

In emergencies, when your body is threatened, a signal can bypass the brain to give extra fast action. This is called a reflex. An example is shown below.

When you touch something hot, your receptor cells send signals up into your spinal cord.

The signals go straight into a motor neuron and back into your arm, relaying a message to your muscles to jerk your arm out of the way.

A message still gets to your brain to tell it what is happening, but only after you are out of danger.

Your sense organs

Your eyes, ears, nose, tongue and skin are your sense organs. They are complicated information collectors that tell you what is happening in the world around you.

Seeing

Each of your eyes is a ball about 2cm across. The picture below shows a cross-section of one eye.

5. The space inside the eyeball is called the chamber: It is filled with clear jelly.

1. The cornea is a clear window that lets light through to the eye.

2. The iris is part of the eye's inner lining, the choroid. The iris is the coloured part you can see.

3. The pupil is a hole in the choroid which lets light in. It expands in dim light and contracts in bright light.

6. The retina is a screen at the back of the eye made up of millions of light-sensitive receptor cells. Your lens focuses an image upside-down on the retina. The receptor cells respond to the light and send messages to the brain, which decodes the signals and works out what you are seeing.

4. The lens is a soft rounded piece of jelly that bends light rays so that they focus into a picture on the back of your eye.

8. All the electrical signals from the retinal receptor cells travel to the brain through the optic nerve.

7. There are two different kinds of retinal receptor cells — rods and cones. Rods react to very dim light but only respond to black and white shades. Cones respond to bright light and also to colours.

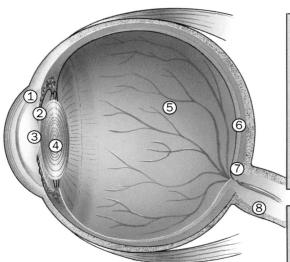

Light rays

Lens focuses rays

Image forms upside-down on the retina.

Hearing

Sounds are very tiny, intense waves in the air. An ear is a sound collector that funnels the waves in through your ear hole to your middle and inner ear.

Inside the ear, the sound waves are amplified and trigger an electrical signal which travels to the brain. The main ear parts are shown below.

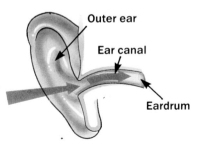

The outer ear, the part that you can see, funnels sound into the ear canal towards the eardrum, positioned in the middle ear. The sound waves make the eardrum vibrate.

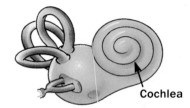

The sound vibrations are passed from the eardrum along two small bones called the hammer and the anvil. They are then passed along a group of three tiny bones called the stirrup.

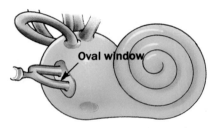

In the inner ear there is a sheet of very thin skin called the 'oval window', stretched over an opening. The bones pass the sound vibrations along to this membrane.

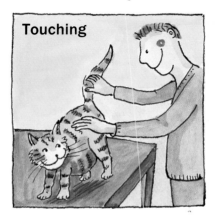

The vibrations then pass into a fluid-filled tube called the cochlea, which is lined with tiny hairs. The vibrations move the hairs and trigger signals which travel to your brain. Your brain then interprets the messages.

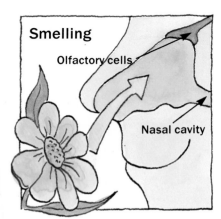

Smelling

Tiny smell molecules enter your nose and stick to the 'olfactory' receptor cells, which then send messages for your brain to decode.

Tasting

All over your tongue there are groups of receptor cells which react to taste. They are gathered into little pits called taste buds.

Touching

Your skin is full of receptor cells, each one sensitive to a particular feeling – such as coldness, heat, softness and pressure.

The brain computer

Your brain is your personal on-board computer, but it is far more complicated than the most powerful computer in existence and no-one yet understands exactly how it works. We only know the basics so far.

What does it do?

Here is a list of the brain's functions:

The brain takes immediate automatic action in case of emergencies such as injury or shock.

The brain stores memories and calls them up when you need them.

The brain keeps your body running smoothly. It constantly gives instructions to all your internal organs to keep them working and makes sure that every part is supplied with enough food, oxygen and warmth.

The brain thinks and makes decisions by taking information from the senses and from memory and combining them to come to a conclusion.

The brain creates emotions such as love, hate, anger and fear.

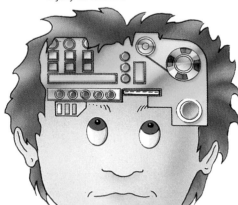

What is the brain?

Your brain is about the same size and shape as a cauliflower. It is soft and pinkish grey, with a wrinkled and folded surface. The largest part of the brain, the cerebral cortex, is split into two halves called hemispheres. Underneath the back of the hemispheres there is a part called the cerebellum, and underneath this there is a brain stem.

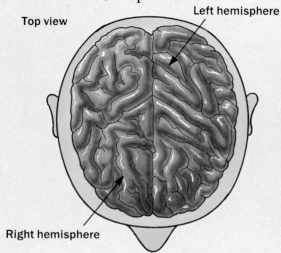

Top view

Left hemisphere

Right hemisphere

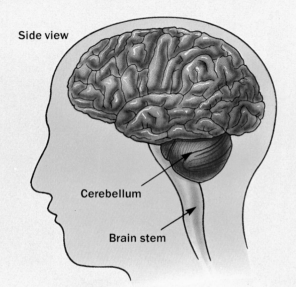

Side view

Cerebellum

Brain stem

How does the brain work?

The brain is made of over ten thousand million neurons (nerve cells), which have lots of tiny branches. These branches connect with other brain neurons in a very complicated way.

One single brain cell may be connected with as many as 25,000 other brain cells! They communicate by passing electrical signals to each other, in the same way as other cells in the nervous system.

The brain map

Particular parts of the body are 'wired up' to particular parts of the brain, called brain centres, which control them. The brain map below shows some of the most important brain centres and the functions they carry out.

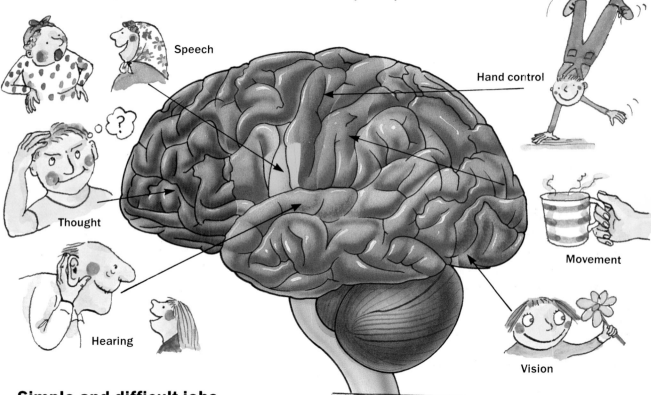

Speech

Hand control

Thought

Movement

Hearing

Vision

Simple and difficult jobs

In parts of the brain which do repetitive tasks, such as keeping the heart beating, the connections between brain cells are quite straightforward. They don't change, since they always do the same job.

In parts of the brain which do complicated tasks, such as remembering and learning, the cells are connected in complicated ways and the patterns of connection can change.

It is thought that the left side of the brain is better at dealing with words and numbers, whereas the right side of the brain is better at creative activities such as painting and music.

Your left brain hemisphere is connected to the right side of your body; your right hemisphere is connected to the left of your body.

Body movement

Your body muscles

There are about 600 different muscles in your body. They move your bones, allowing you to bend your joints.

They also help to keep all your internal organs, such as your heart, working properly.

Muscle movement

The muscles that you use for moving your body limbs are called skeletal muscles.

They are controlled by the conscious part of your brain, so you can move them whenever you choose.

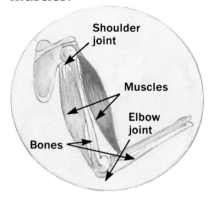

A muscle is joined to two bones. It can move one bone towards or away from another. They bend at the joint between them.

Muscles pull on the bones they are attached to by tensing themselves so that they grow shorter and fatter.

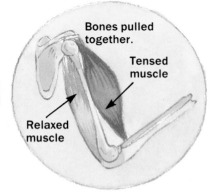

Muscles can't push, so they must work in pairs. Each muscle in a pair pulls in a different direction when it tenses.

Feeling them work

You can feel how muscles work together by bending your arm.

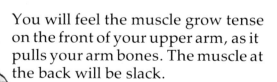

You will feel the muscle grow tense on the front of your upper arm, as it pulls your arm bones. The muscle at the back will be slack.

Unbend your arm. You will feel the muscle at the front relax, while the muscle at the back grows tense, pulling your arm the other way.

What are muscles made of?

Electron micrograph picture of a skeletal muscle fibre.

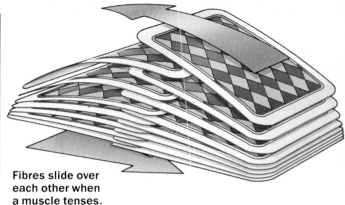

Fibres slide over each other when a muscle tenses.

Muscle looks like meat (in fact, most cuts of meat are made of animal muscle). Each muscle is made from bundles of fibres together with lots of nerves which give the muscle signals to tense. There are also lots of blood vessels.

In a muscle, millions of tiny fibres are lined up in rows. There are two different sorts of fibres. When a muscle tenses, the two sets slide over each other, like two packs of cards being pushed together. This makes the muscle shorter and fatter.

Muscle facts

Some muscles work all the time. For instance, your heart muscles work constantly. Muscles of this type have a special arrangement of fibres that stops them ever getting tired.

The bulkiest muscles in your body are the two gluteus maximi in your buttocks. The smallest muscle is the stapedius in your ear. It is only about 1mm long!

Muscles are joined to bones by tendons, flexible cables that can be quite long. For instance, your fingers are attached by tendons to muscles in your forearm.

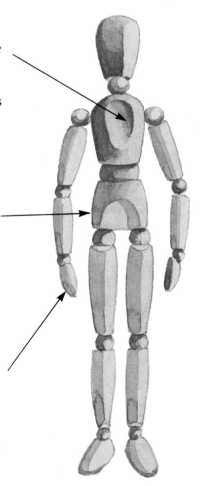

Tiredness and exercise

When you tense a muscle, it uses up energy and makes waste products. When the waste builds up, it stops the muscle fibres working properly and your muscle gets tired.

Exercise triggers muscles to make more fibres and grow stronger. You lose fibres if you don't exercise.

Your skeleton

You have 206 bones which make up your skeleton. It gives your body shape, allows you to move and protects your internal organs.

All your most important organs are protected by bone. For instance, your brain is covered by your skull, and your heart and lungs by your ribs.

Skeleton map

Bones come in lots of different shapes and sizes, as shown below.

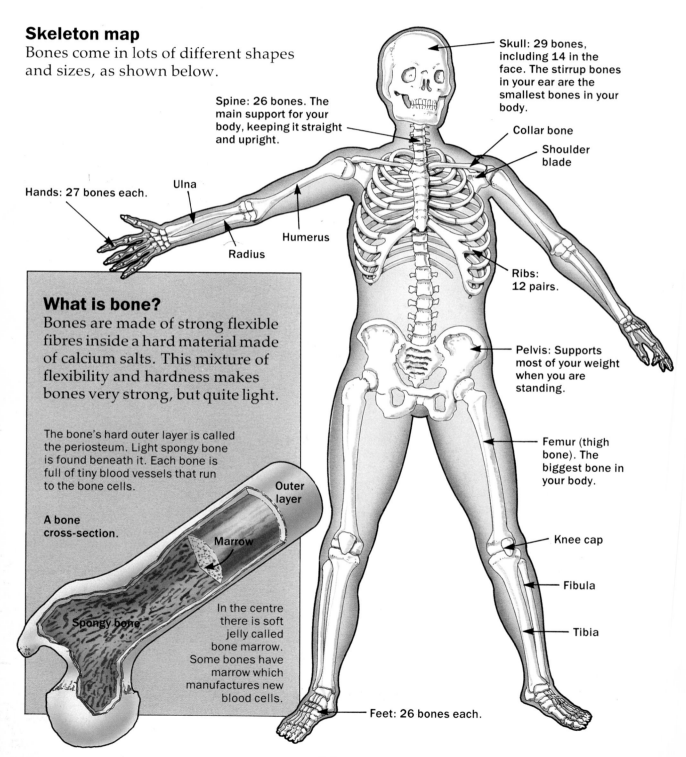

Spine: 26 bones. The main support for your body, keeping it straight and upright.

Hands: 27 bones each.

Ulna

Humerus

Radius

Skull: 29 bones, including 14 in the face. The stirrup bones in your ear are the smallest bones in your body.

Collar bone

Shoulder blade

Ribs: 12 pairs.

Pelvis: Supports most of your weight when you are standing.

Femur (thigh bone). The biggest bone in your body.

Knee cap

Fibula

Tibia

Feet: 26 bones each.

What is bone?

Bones are made of strong flexible fibres inside a hard material made of calcium salts. This mixture of flexibility and hardness makes bones very strong, but quite light.

The bone's hard outer layer is called the periosteum. Light spongy bone is found beneath it. Each bone is full of tiny blood vessels that run to the bone cells.

A bone cross-section.

Outer layer

Marrow

Spongy bone

In the centre there is soft jelly called bone marrow. Some bones have marrow which manufactures new blood cells.

How do bones grow?

Near the ends of each growing bone there are bands made of flexible fibre called cartilage. The bone cells in these bands multiply to grow more cartilage, making the bone gradually longer.

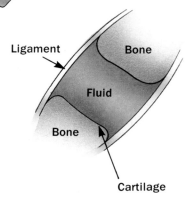

Cartilage bands

The bendy part of your nose is made of cartilage.

By the time a person is 25 years old all the bands of cartilage have hardened, so growth finishes. However, the process can start up again to mend breaks.

Holding bones together

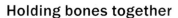

Skull bones fit together like a jigsaw.

Ligament

Bone

Fluid

Bone

Cartilage

The place where two bones meet is called a joint. Where bones don't need to move, they simply fit together like jigsaw pieces. However, in most places, bones need to be able to move at their joints.

The bone tips in a joint are covered with protective cartilage. The two ends are held together by a wrapping of tough, stretchy ligament, which holds some fluid in between the bones.

Types of joint

In ball and socket joints, one bone forms a hole and one bone forms a peg that can swivel about. In hinge joints, one bone slides over the other in one direction only.

Ball and socket

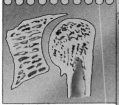

Hinge joint

The spine locks

The 26 bones of your spine are held in place by little projections which lock together. Small cushions of cartilage sit between each bone to make movement smooth.

As you walk around during the day, the cartilage cushions are squashed down by your weight. So in the evening you are about 1cm shorter than when you woke up! The cushions soon spring back up again.

Cartilage

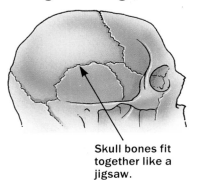

Active astronauts

When you put regular stress on your bones, they strengthen. But if there are few stresses, the bones weaken and their calcium ebbs away.

The first space astronauts found that their bones weakened when they spent some time weightless in space (although things got back to normal when they returned to Earth). Now astronauts do lots of exercises while they are in space to keep their skeletons healthy.

Your heart and lungs

Blood is your body's transport system. It flows to all your cells, carrying food and oxygen. It is constantly pumped by the heart through a network of tubes called blood vessels, which reach every part of the body.

The hardworking heart

Your heart is a hollow ball made of muscle and filled with blood. It is situated in the middle of your chest, leaning slightly to your left. As it pumps, it squeezes blood out into the blood vessels.

The heart beats about 100,000 times a day, and it never gets tired! It is controlled by nerves that never switch off. They carry messages from your brain to keep the heart beating.

The blood route

Blood travels through about 96,558 km of blood vessels, the equivalent of a quarter of the way to the moon!

There are three different kinds of blood vessels, each one doing a different job.

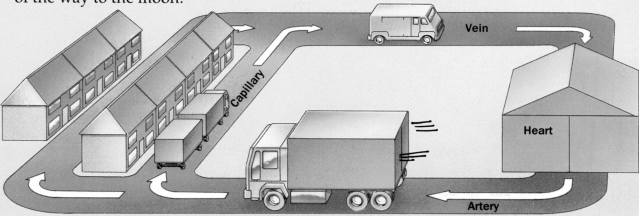

Your arteries are the 'motorways' for your blood. They carry it from the heart to all parts of the body — and they do it quickly! They have thick muscular walls to contain the fast-moving blood.

When arteries reach organs or muscles, they branch into tiny vessels called capillaries, which carry blood past each cell like country roads carrying slow traffic past every house.

The cells take what they need from the blood and dump their waste back into it. The capillaries join up again into thin tubes called veins, which carry the blood very slowly back to the heart.

Inside the heart

The heart is divided into two halves by a wall. Each half is made up of two chambers, an atrium and a ventricle.

The two chambers have a one-way door between them. The blood travels through this one-way system.

1. A large vein called the vena cava carries blood to the heart collected from all parts of the body except the lungs.

3. The right atrium pushes blood into the right ventricle, which has thick muscular walls.

5. The pulmonary vein carries blood away from the lungs back to the left atrium of the heart.

7. The left ventricle sends blood to the left aorta, which delivers it to your arteries.

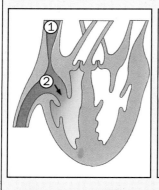 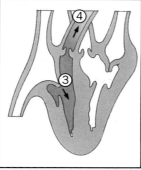 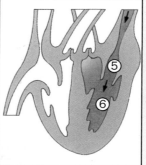 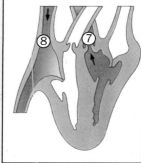

2. The blood from the vena cava enters the right atrium, which has thin walls.

4. The right ventricle pushes blood into the pulmonary artery, which takes it to the lungs.

6. The left atrium pushes blood into the left ventricle, which has thick muscular walls.

8. Once the blood has been round the body, veins carry it back to the vena cava.

All about blood

Not everyone's blood is the same. There are four different sorts, called blood groups: A, B, AB and O. Blood contains its own cells, which are designed to do particular jobs for the body.

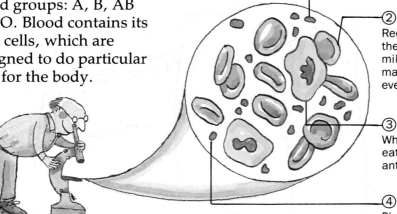

① Plasma is the liquid part of blood. It is made of water and dissolved food nutrients.

② Red blood cells carry oxygen around the body. There are about 200 million in a drop of blood, and you make about 140 million new ones every minute!

③ White blood cells fight diseases by eating bacteria and making antibodies that kill viruses.

④ Platelets are tiny pieces of cells that help to clot blood when you cut yourself.

Why you breathe

Your body cells need food to give them energy, but they also need oxygen to release the energy, in the same way that a fire needs air to make heat and light.

Oxygen comes from the air. When you breathe oxygen in, it travels deep into your lungs, where it is absorbed into your blood and gets taken to your body cells.

What happens when you breathe

The respiratory centre is the part of your brain that tells your body when to breathe. When you are at rest, it makes you breathe 10-14 times a minute. When you exercise, it may tell your body to breathe up to 75 times a minute!

Air goes into your body through your nose and mouth. Inside the nose there are hairs and a sticky substance called mucus. These trap dirt and dust. Mucus and blood vessels in the nose warm and moisten the air.

Air enters the larynx (the 'voicebox') through an opening called the glottis, which is closed off when you swallow food.

The air goes down through the trachea, or windpipe, which is protected by hard bands of gristle called cartilage.

The trachea divides into two tubes called bronchi, one going to each lung. Inside the lungs, they branch out, forming much smaller airways called bronchioles.

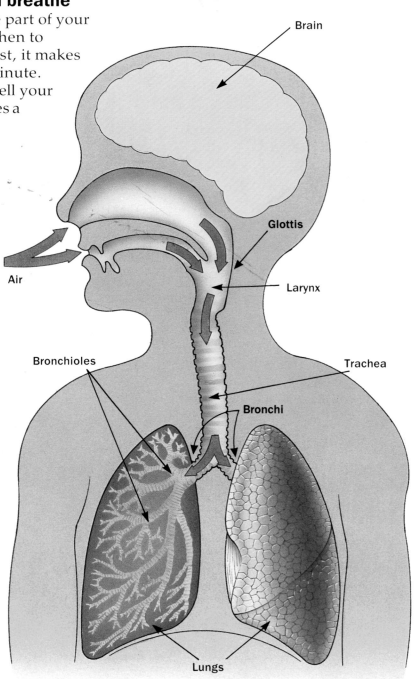

Brain

Glottis

Air

Larynx

Bronchioles

Trachea

Bronchi

Lungs

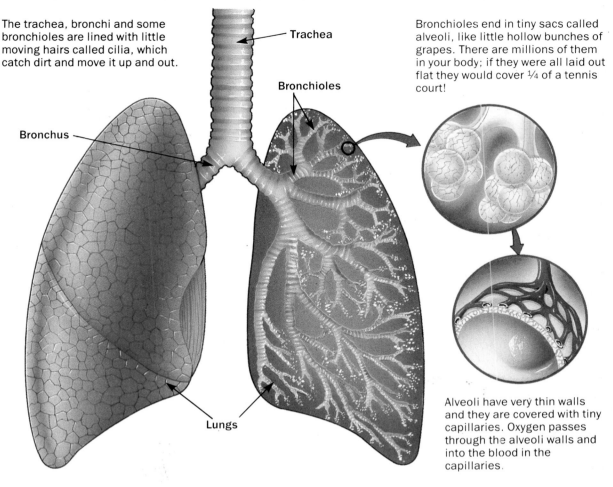

The trachea, bronchi and some bronchioles are lined with little moving hairs called cilia, which catch dirt and move it up and out.

Trachea

Bronchioles

Bronchus

Lungs

Bronchioles end in tiny sacs called alveoli, like little hollow bunches of grapes. There are millions of them in your body; if they were all laid out flat they would cover ¼ of a tennis court!

Alveoli have very thin walls and they are covered with tiny capillaries. Oxygen passes through the alveoli walls and into the blood in the capillaries.

The lungs are spongy masses of air tubes and blood vessels.

When cells use oxygen to burn food, they make a waste gas called carbon dioxide. It is dumped into the blood and travels to the lungs, where it passes out of the blood in the capillaries, through the alveoli walls, and out of the lungs.

How do you breathe?

When you breathe, your chest is moved in and out by the muscles between your ribs.

The space inside your chest is also made bigger and smaller by your diaphragm, which is the floor of your chest. When you breathe in, it moves down; when you breathe out, it moves up.

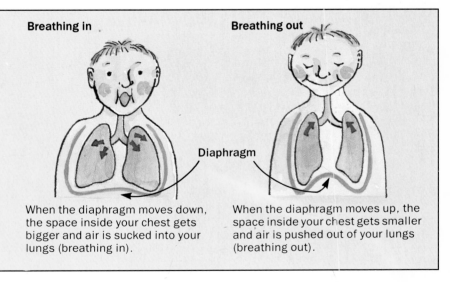

Breathing in

Breathing out

Diaphragm

When the diaphragm moves down, the space inside your chest gets bigger and air is sucked into your lungs (breathing in).

When the diaphragm moves up, the space inside your chest gets smaller and air is pushed out of your lungs (breathing out).

Eating and living

Your body needs the food you eat in order to survive. Food gives you the energy to run about, the capacity to repair cuts, and the capacity to grow.

Your body gradually breaks up food into separate parts, called nutrients. Each nutrient is used for a different purpose, as shown below.

Food nutrients

The nutrients in packaged foods are usually listed. The nutrient amounts shown on this page are from the label on a typical baked bean tin.

Energy per tin:
689kJ/162kcal

9000kJ

Energy

Every day your body needs a certain amount of energy, measured in kilojoules or kilocalories (kJ or kcal). The figures on the bean tin label show the amount of energy that the nutrients in all the beans will give you.

The amount of daily energy you need depends on your age, sex, size and how active you are. For instance, a 12-14 year old girl needs 9000kJ and a boy of the same age needs 11000kJ.

11000kJ

Protein

Your body can use protein for energy, although it is quite low in kJ/kcals. However, its main use is for the repair, growth and smooth running of your body parts. You can get protein from foods such as fish, meat, cheese, eggs, beans and lentils.

Protein per serving 11.3g.

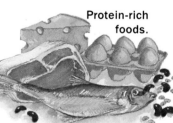

Protein-rich foods.

Carbohydrates

Carbohydrates are high in kJ/kcals. Their main function is to provide energy, so the amount you need depends on how active you are. If you eat more than you can use, your body stores the excess as fat. You can get carbohydrates from bread, potatoes, pasta, rice, flour and sugar.

Carbohydrates per serving 29.5g of which sugars 13.5g.

Carbohydrate-rich foods.

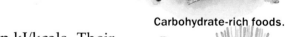

Fats

Fats have high levels of kJ/kcals. The body uses them for energy and to build cell walls. You need very little fat, and it is better to get your energy from carbohydrates. Large amounts of 'saturated' fats, found in animal products, can cause heart disease, so it is better to eat 'unsaturated' fats found in vegetable oil and margarine. Fat-rich foods include dairy products, meat, oil and nuts.

Fat per serving 0.7g of which saturates 0.2g.

Fat-rich foods.

Sodium

Salt's scientific name is sodium chloride. The amount shown on the tin label is the sodium content of the salt.

   You need sodium in small amounts, but too much causes high blood pressure. You can get enough sodium from food without adding any extra.

Vitamins

Your body needs 13 chemicals called vitamins to keep it healthy. For instance, vitamin C is needed for resisting disease and vitamin A is good for your eyesight.

Minerals

You need small amounts of minerals such as calcium and iron. Calcium is used by your body for making and clotting blood and making bone. Iron is needed for healthy blood.

Sodium per serving 1.1g.

Dietary fibre per serving 16.4g.

FIBRE
CALCIUM
IRON
VITAMIN C
VITAMIN A
VITAMIN B
VITAMIN D

Dietary fibre

Your guts need something to squeeze on in order to move food along and extract nutrients (see page 24). Fibre is used for this purpose. It is indigestible material that passes through your stomach unchanged; but without it you would soon get constipated.

Water

Your body is ¾ water! Without water you could not survive. You can get a regular supply by eating and drinking.

Eating what you need

You can't spend every meal with a calculator, trying to work out if you are getting all the nutrients you need!

All you have to do is eat enough of the right kinds of food in your daily diet. That way you get sufficient supplies of nutrients for your body's needs.

It's easy for babies!

Young babies only need to drink their mother's milk. It contains all the nutrients they need in order to grow, together with antibodies which fight infection. There's more about it on page 43.

Older babies, children and adults need much more food. At about five or six months old, babies begin to eat solids.

Food you should avoid

Many ready-made snacks and packaged meals contain lots of carbohydrate and fat, but very little fibre, vitamins or minerals. These foods may make you feel full but they don't provide your body with all the supplies it needs in order to stay healthy.

Snack foods such as those shown below often have chemicals added to make them taste good, even though they contain few nutrients and are not good for your body.

Chips

Cake

Crisps

Chocolate

Biscuits

What you should eat

By eating lots of different unprocessed foods, you can make sure that your body gets all it needs. Here is a basic plan for a healthy diet.

Eat foods from all the boxes every day, but try to stick to items shown in the ticked lists rather than items shown in the crossed lists.

Carbohydrates

EAT THESE...
Brown bread, pasta, brown rice, potatoes in their jackets, bran-rich cereals.

...INSTEAD OF THESE
White bread, chips, sweets, biscuits, cakes, crisps.

Protein

EAT THESE...
Fish, beans, chicken, lean meat, low fat cheese.

...INSTEAD OF THESE
Fatty meat, hard cheese, eggs.

Fat

EAT THESE...
Small amounts of vegetable margarine and oils.

...INSTEAD OF THESE
Butter, eggs, cheese, fatty meat and fried food.

Vitamins and minerals

EAT THESE...
Fresh fruit (such as apples, oranges, pears etc.) Fresh or frozen vegetables (such as carrots, courgettes, leeks, tomatoes, spinach, broccoli etc.)

Unhealthy diets

 A diet low in vitamins causes bleeding gums, slow healing of wounds and poor night vision.

 A diet high in fat and sugar can lead to obesity, heart disease and chronic constipation.

 Too much salt can cause high blood pressure and heart disease.

A lesson from Henry

The English Tudor King Henry VIII was a legendary big eater. But historians now think that he actually died from diet deficiencies!

Henry ate lots of meat but very few vegetables (they were only thought fit for peasants in his time). He developed the symptoms of scurvy, a disease caused by lack of vitamin C.

Using food

The nutrients in the food you eat must be adapted for use by your body. You need to 'digest' the food, breaking it up into building blocks which your body can rebuild into the nutrients it needs to keep functioning.

Digestion — from start to finish

Food makes a long journey through your body, as shown below.

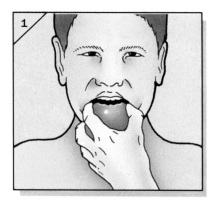

The teeth at the front of your mouth bite off a piece of food. Your tongue and lips push it to the side of the mouth to be crushed by the back teeth. The food is chewed and mixed with saliva, which contains an enzyme that begins to break down the carbohydrate.

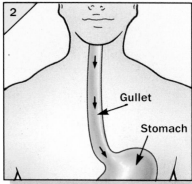

When you swallow, the food is pushed down into your gullet (or oesophagus). Muscles squeeze it down like toothpaste in a tube. It enters the stomach through a ring of muscle which normally holds the stomach shut rather like a purse string.

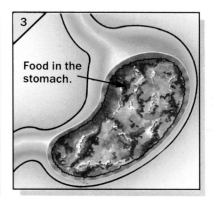

The muscles in the stomach squeeze the food and mix it up with gastric juice. This substance contains an enzyme which breaks down proteins, together with an acid which kills off any germs that you might have swallowed. The resulting mixture of food and gastric juice is called chyme.

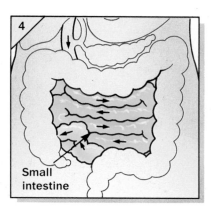

After about an hour, the chyme is squirted out of the stomach into the small intestine. Here it is mixed with more digestive juices which break down carbohydrates into sugars, proteins into amino acids and fats into fatty acids.

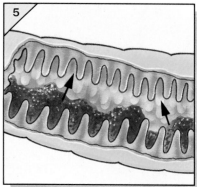

The wall of the small intestine looks like a mass of tiny fingers. These contain blood and lymph vessels covered by a thin membrane. Lymph is a clear liquid that does lots of jobs in the body. Fatty acids dissolve into it through the intestine wall.

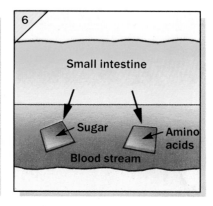

Sugar and amino acids dissolve into the blood through the intestine wall. The blood travels to the liver, which stores the nutrients or sends them where they are needed. The fatty acids in the lymph join the blood at a vessel in the neck.

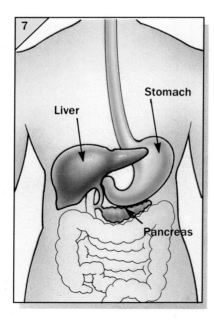

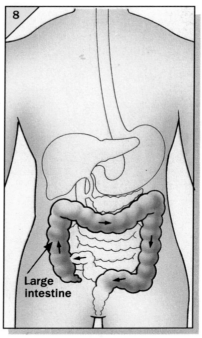

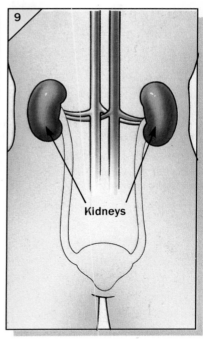

The liver stores and sends out glucose, a simple sugar made from carbohydrates. An organ called the pancreas checks the amount of glucose in the blood. If the level gets too low or too high, it makes hormones that trigger the liver to correct the balance.

The food has now had most of its nutrients taken out. It goes from the small intestine into the large intestine, where any minerals and water left in it dissolve into the blood through the intestine wall.

Your body cells throw away waste materials into your blood. It has to be constantly cleaned by the kidneys, which also make sure that the blood has enough water and salt in it.

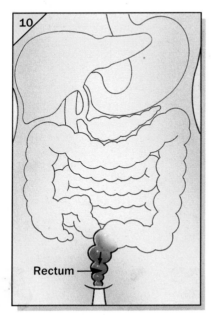

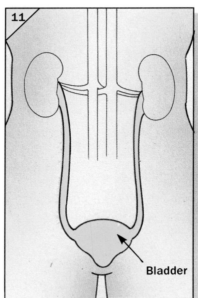

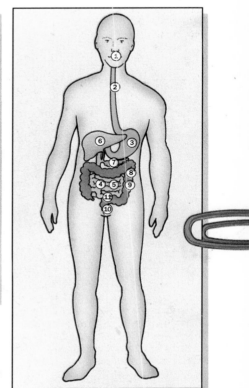

By the time the food gets to the rectum, all that is left is fibre, which the body cannot digest. When you go to the lavatory, the fibre is squeezed out of the anus as solid waste matter, called faeces.

All the waste material from your body cells is dissolved into water to make a mixture called urine. It runs out of the kidneys into the bladder, where it is stored until you go to the lavatory.

Skin, hair, teeth and nails

Your skin is the best suit of clothes you will ever have! It fits you perfectly, whatever size you grow to.

It keeps you warm or cool; it's washable, lasts a lifetime, and gathers character with age!

Versatile skin

The average adult has about 2 sq.m of skin. It varies in thickness on the body, but it is never more than 5mm thick.

Skin varies in form, too. For instance, the skin on your elbows is loose, to allow for bending, whereas the skin on your foot soles is firm and ridged, which helps your feet to grip.

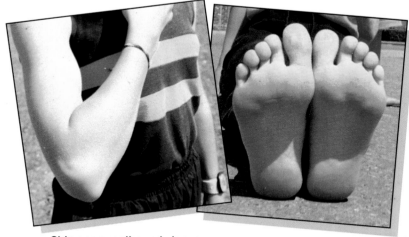

Skin on your elbows is loose.

Skin on your foot soles is rigid and firm.

Skin structure

The picture below shows a cross-section of skin.

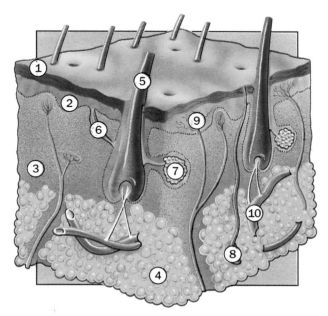

1. The epidermis is the top layer. It is made of flat, dead cells that are constantly worn away. They are waterproof and protect the skin from damage.

2. Next comes a section of living cells, which constantly divide to make more cells for the top layer.

3. The dermis layer is made of elastic strands that give skin its stretchiness.

4. A fat layer provides insulation and protection.

5. Hair follicles produce the hairs that cover the skin.

6. Each hair has a muscle to make it stand erect or lie flat.

7. Oil glands produce oil to keep the skin supple and waterproof.

8. Sweat glands produce watery salty sweat to cool the body. Apocrine sweat glands, under the arms and round the genitals, produce a more milky liquid with a strong smell.

9. There are lots of nerve endings ('sensory receptors') of all sorts. They are sensitive to things like cold, warmth, pressure and pain (see page 6).

10. Blood vessels keep the skin supplied with food and oxygen.

Skin protection

Skin is a barrier against poisons and disease. It keeps most things out; only a couple of toxic metals and plant poisons can penetrate the surface. Diseases can only get in where the skin is broken.

Keeping cool

When your skin gets hot, its blood vessels expand, bringing blood close to the skin surface where it can be cooled down by the air. Sweat also takes heat away when it evaporates.

Your skin sweats more when you are warm.

Keeping warm

When skin gets cold, its blood vessels close down to keep your warm blood deep beneath the surface. The hair muscles also tense to make the hairs stand on end, trapping a layer of warm air close to the skin.

When your skin hairs stand on end, you get 'goosepimples'.

Oh no, B.O.!

Your apocrine sweat glands, under your arms and around your genitals, produce sweat that is very attractive to bacteria. If you don't wash regularly, the bacteria will grow in it and produce a 'pongy armpits' smell!

Skin colour

Skin contains a coloured substance called melanin, which ranges in tone from yellowy-brown to black.

The amount of melanin you have affects your skin colour. Dark-skinned people have lots of melanin, whereas fair-skinned people have very little.

Melanin protects skin from harmful sun rays. The skin makes more protective melanin when strong sunlight shines on it, which is why people tan. If the skin doesn't make enough melanin, painful sunburn ensues!

That's my skin!

Your skin cells are constantly being worn away and replaced. Most house dust is actually made from flakes of dead skin which have rubbed off peoples' bodies!

All about hair

Your hair, nails and teeth are all 'external' parts of your body, which you can see. It is important that you take care of them.

Hair structure

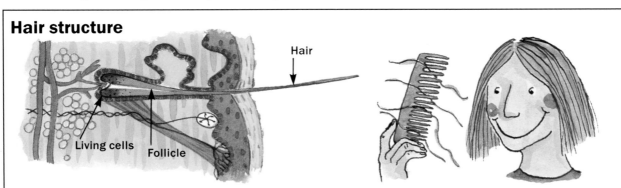

Living cells

Follicle

Hair

Each hair is rooted into the skin inside a tube called a follicle (see p.26). At the base of the follicle there are cells which make the hair from a protein called keratin. The hair itself is dead, although the cells that make it are alive.

Follicle cells keep a hair growing for a certain length of time and then stop. They begin to make a new hair, which pushes the old one out. A hair on your head may last up to 15 years, but an eyelash hair lasts only six months.

Caring for your hair

During the years of puberty, your hair may get more greasy than usual. You can wash it as much as you like, but try to use a mild shampoo.

Dandruff is a build-up of dead skin cells stuck together with grease. You can remove it by washing your hair regularly with a gentle shampoo.

Split ends are caused by rough brushing or using a hairdryer that is too hot.

You can prevent split hairs spreading by having your hair trimmed every two months. Try not to use a hairdryer too much.

28

All about nails

Just like hair, your nails are dead cells made from keratin. They grow from the base, the white half-moon. Unlike hairs they grow continuously, about 4cm a year, and they don't drop off to be replaced.

Cut your nails in a gentle oval, level with your fingertips. It is best to use nail clippers or curved nail scissors. You can file off any rough edges with an emery board.

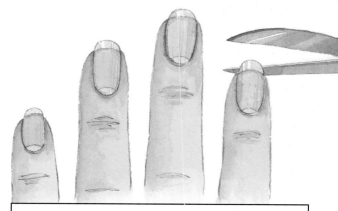

Don't bite your nails! It weakens them and transfers dirt and germs into your mouth.

All about teeth

Your teeth break up food ready to be digested. A tooth has a complicated structure, shown below.

1. Dentine is a hard substance that forms most of the tooth.

2. The root is the part of the tooth that is stuck in your jaw.

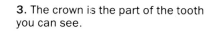

3. The crown is the part of the tooth you can see.

4. The tooth is covered with a shiny hard coating called enamel, made of calcium and phosphorus.

5. The soft core is called pulp. It is made of cells, nerves and blood vessels.

Different teeth

You have three different kinds of teeth.

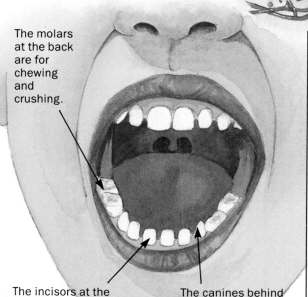

The molars at the back are for chewing and crushing.

The incisors at the front are for cutting food.

The canines behind are for tearing and piercing.

Caring for your teeth

Many people over the age of 40 have no teeth left! You can help prevent this happening to you by looking after your teeth properly.

Teeth are covered in bacteria. Every time you eat something sweet, the bacteria multiply, producing acid which causes the teeth to decay.

If you brush your teeth every day, especially after meals, you will get rid of some of the bacteria. Visit a dentist regularly for a check-up.

Growing up

You grow and develop very fast in the first few years of life. The second period of fast development begins when you are about 12.

This stage is called 'puberty', and lasts until you are about 18. During this time, you develop an adult body which can produce babies.

Girls' puberty changes

The skin makes more sweat, so sometimes the skin pores get clogged up and spots occur.

The breasts begin to grow and develop so that they will be able to make milk to feed a baby.

Wiry thick hair grows under the arms and around the vagina area, where it is called pubic hair.

The hips grow wider, to allow room for a baby to grow inside the body.

Periods start. Blood comes out of the vagina for about 5 days every month (see page 33). This happens from puberty until a woman is about 50. It stops during pregnancy.

Guide to growth

Six months

Six years

During the first 18 years of life, the human body grows all the time and gradually becomes adult. The sequence on the right is a rough guide to childhood growth stages.

Babies can sit up, hold objects, smile and recognise people. But they can't talk, walk or feed themselves, and they rely completely on adults. They grow about 20cm a year.

Six-year-old children can run, climb, talk and feed themselves. They can learn to read and write, but they still rely on adults a lot. They grow about 8cm a year.

Boys' puberty changes

The larynx (the 'voice box') gets bigger. This causes the voice to 'break', which means it gets deeper in tone.

Wiry hair grows under the arms and around the penis (where it is called pubic hair). Hair begins to grow on the face and sometimes on the chest, legs and back. For our early ancestors, who didn't wear clothes, this hair growth may have been an important signal of male maturity.

Both boys and girls get taller and heavier during puberty. On average, boys grow taller than girls.

When the penis is touched or stroked it grows bigger and becomes hard and erect because it is pumped full of blood. Occasionally you may get a 'spontaneous erection', which happens on its own without warning.

The skin begins to make more sweat, so boys may become prone to spots.

The muscles in the body get bigger and stronger.

A white sticky liquid called semen can come out of the penis when it is erect. This is called ejaculation. Semen is made by the body's glands, including the testicles, which are two soft pouches behind the penis.

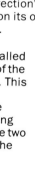

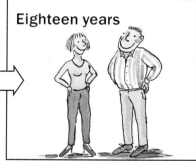

Twelve years

Eighteen years

Twelve-year-olds can do most of the things that adults can do. But they still lack experience and confidence, so they need adults to provide protection and advice.

Eighteen-year-olds have reached adulthood. Their bodies are adult in shape and appearance and their sexual parts are fully developed.

Don't worry!

There is no right or wrong way for puberty changes to happen, because everyone is different. Some people start puberty at 9, some at 16. In some people, the changes occur quite quickly; in others they may take several years. Everyone gets there in the end!

Knowing your body — GIRLS

It will help you not to worry if you know what is happening to your body when it is changing during puberty.

On these two pages you can find out what changes happen on the outside and the inside of a girl's body.

Changes on the outside

The picture below shows the female sex organs positioned between the legs. Together they are called the vulva. Don't worry if yours look different; they vary from person to person.

1. Mons: A mound of fat covering the pubic bone. During puberty pubic hair begins to grow over this area.

2. Outer labia: These are two soft, thick 'lips', with pubic hair growing on them. They protect the inner parts of the vulva. Touching can make them swell and stand out a little bit. During puberty they may begin to grow bigger.

3. Inner labia: These lips are thinner than the outer labia, and they are very sensitive to touch. The left and right labia are usually different sizes.

4. Urinary opening: This is the opening of the urethra, a tube leading up to your bladder. The opening is where urine comes out.

5. Clitoris: This is rather like a small button with a hood on it. It is extremely sensitive, and its purpose is simply to make you feel good when it is stroked.

6. Vaginal opening: The opening to the vagina, a tube leading to the internal sex organs. Blood comes out of here during a period, and a man's penis fits in here during sex.

7. Hymen: This is a thin skin layer partly covering the vaginal opening. It may gradually stretch and break as you grow. Otherwise it is harmlessly broken during first sexual intercourse.

8. Anus: The opening where faeces leave the body. It is held tight most of the time by a ring of muscles.

Changes on the inside

This picture shows the female sex organs inside the body. They grow bigger during puberty.

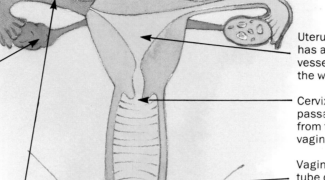

Ovaries: There are two of these, one on each side of the body. They contain thousands of tiny eggs (rather like little bags of jelly) called ova. Each ovum is even smaller in size than a full stop!

An ovum can grow into a baby if it is joined with a man's sperm.

Fallopian tubes: These 12cm-long tubes link the ovaries and the uterus.

Uterus: This muscular bag has a thick lining of blood vessels. It is also called the womb.

Cervix: This narrow passageway is the opening from the uterus into the vagina.

Vagina: This is a muscular tube connecting the uterus with the outside of the body. Inside the vagina there are glands which produce a cleansing lubricating liquid.

The menstrual cycle

Until a girl reaches puberty, her eggs stay dormant in her ovaries.

Once the puberty stage arrives, an egg ripens in an ovary each month.

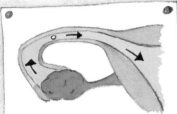

About 14 days before a period, a ripe egg is released from an ovary and travels down a fallopian tube towards the uterus.

Whilst the egg travels down, the uterus lining thickens with blood. If the egg is fertilized, it will stick here.

If the egg is not fertilized, the uterus lining breaks down and comes out through the vagina during a period.

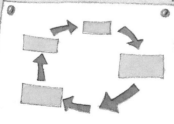

The whole process is called the menstrual cycle. Every month an egg grows, and if it is not fertilized you will have your period.

When they first start, your periods may not be regular. Eventually they usually come once every 20 to 36 days and last from two to six days.

Knowing your body — BOYS

Some of the changes that occur during puberty can be difficult for boys to cope with at first. But there is really no need to worry!

The things that are happening to you are completely normal. The changes signal that you are becoming a grown man.

Changes on the outside

The picture below shows the sex organs that can be found on the outside of a man's body, between the legs. These organs grow larger during puberty.

1. Penis: At the tip of the penis there is an opening where both urine and semen come out. The penis is very sensitive, especially at the tip, called the glans.

2. Foreskin: This protects the penis, but is pushed back when the penis is erect. Some people have the foreskin removed, for religious or health reasons. This is called circumcision. Dirt is easily trapped under the foreskin so you need to wash it thoroughly.

3. Glands. Underneath the foreskin there are glands which produce a creamy, white substance called smegma. This helps the foreskin to glide back smoothly over the tip of the penis.

4. Scrotum: This soft, loose bag of skin holds two testicles, or testes, inside. These make sperm, part of the semen that comes out during ejaculation. They can only do their job if they are cool; that's why they are held outside the body.

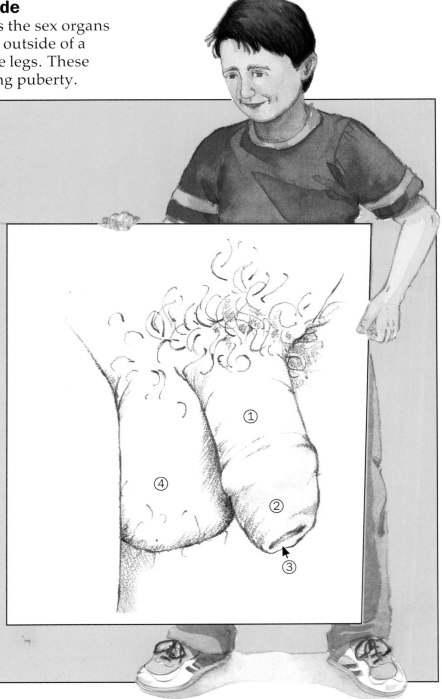

Changes on the inside

This picture shows the male sex organs positioned inside the body.

These organs grow larger and develop during puberty.

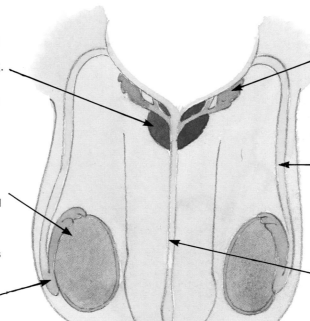

Prostate gland: This gland produces a liquid that helps sperm to move along.

The testes: These begin to make sperm some time between the ages of 10 and 16. Several million sperm are produced every day, but each one is very tiny.

The testes also produce a male sex hormone called testosterone. This acts as a kind of chemical messenger. It travels round the body and triggers off puberty changes.

Epididymis: This coiled tube lies over the back of each testis. Sperm are stored here.

Seminal vesicles: These glands produce a liquid that nourishes sperm.

Sperm ducts: These two tubes connect the epididymis to the urethra. When a man ejaculates, sperm shoot out of the epididymis into the sperm ducts, and out of the penis via the urethra. The sperm is mixed with nourishing liquids on the way, to make semen.

Urethra: This tube is connected to the bladder and carries urine outside the body. When a man ejaculates, it only carries semen.

Sperm count

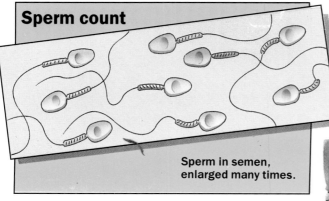

Sperm in semen, enlarged many times.

Only about a teaspoonful of semen comes out of the penis during ejaculation. Yet this small amount contains over 300 million sperm!

There is no regular cycle of male sperm-making, as there is with female egg-releasing. Sperm are made all the time, from puberty onwards.

Wet dreams

Occasionally, you may find that you have ejaculated in your sleep. This is called a 'wet dream', and is quite common during the years of puberty. It happens because your body hasn't yet got used to a new way of working.

Feeling different

Growing up isn't just about how your body develops or what it does. It's also about how you feel.

Highs and lows

In both boys and girls, hormones act as chemical messengers that tell your body to grow and develop during puberty. They act on your emotions, too. You may find that your moods go up and down like a yoyo! Don't worry about this; your hormones and your moods will settle down eventually.

The one and only you!

The changes in the way your body looks may make you feel very shy and awkward. For instance, you may be worried that you aren't growing enough or that you are developing too early.

You may want to be bigger, smaller, thinner, fatter, taller – or just perfect! Well, don't forget that everyone develops at their own rate, and there is no set 'right' size or shape for any part of you.

Using your brain

As you get older, you will be allowed to do more on your own. Your parents will see that you are growing up and becoming more responsible, so you will be allowed more freedom.

You will have to start making decisions for yourself.

Some problems solved

Here are some common questions about aspects of puberty, along with some helpful answers.

How do I cope with my period?

You lose a couple of tablespoons of blood during a period. There are two different ways of catching it; what you use is up to you.

Sanitary towels have a sticky backing which fits on to pants.

You can put tampons in your vagina. It is quite easy to do, and simple instructions come with the packets.

You may get an ache in your tummy or in the lower part of your back when you have your period. This is because your uterus is working hard to push the blood out. You can help to ease the pain with gentle exercise or a hot water bottle placed on your back or stomach.

Some women suffer from pre-menstrual tension just before a period. This is due to hormones, and it can cause spots, headaches and depression. It is difficult to prevent PMT, but once you are aware of the reasons for it, it becomes easier to cope with.

Is my penis too small?

Penis size varies. The size of your penis bears no relation to its erect size, and has no effect on lovemaking.

Should I touch myself?

It doesn't do any harm to touch your genitals. This is not something you need to worry about.

Celebrate!

Puberty is the fanfare for the beginning of your adult life. It is a very exciting time, and in many cultures it is treated as a big event!

Pregnancy and birth

If a man and woman want a baby, the sperm has to get all the way from the man's testicles into the woman's womb. This happens when a man and a woman have sexual intercourse. Most people call it 'making love', because it is something that happens when two people love each other.

Making love

Most people begin to make love by kissing and stroking. They want to be as close as possible to each other.

It often happens in bed, because that is a warm and comfortable place to relax in.

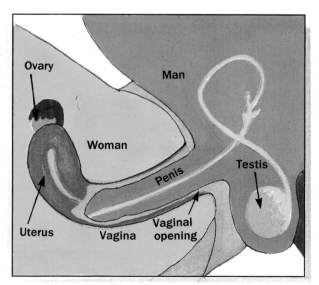

The man's penis fits comfortably inside the woman's vagina through her vaginal opening, which is behind her urinary opening (see p.32).

During lovemaking, the woman's clitoris becomes very sensitive and enjoys being stroked. The man has an erection; his penis becomes stiffer and longer. The woman's vagina becomes bigger and slippery, so the penis can fit inside it.

When a man and a woman make love, the feeling is very nice, and they move their hips to make the feeling even better. In the end, the feeling is so good that the woman's clitoris has a wonderful experience called an orgasm, which makes her feel good all over. The man's orgasm is in his penis, when the sperm rush up into the vagina. He feels good all over, too.

Egg + sperm = baby

Once the sperm get inside the vagina, they must find the egg. So, working as a team, millions of them race together up the vagina to the womb. If the egg is not there, they carry on into the fallopian tubes. Many sperm don't complete the journey, but some finally meet the egg.

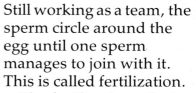

Still working as a team, the sperm circle around the egg until one sperm manages to join with it. This is called fertilization.

The fertilized egg finds a place to settle in the soft coating of the womb, and the new baby has now begun.

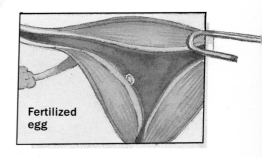

Fertilized egg

Contraception

Making love is so nice that most couples want to do it often; but they don't always want to start a baby. They may use contraceptives to prevent this.

Some people don't like to use contraceptives, for religious or other reasons. Every couple must do what they feel happiest and most comfortable with.

There are lots of different forms of contraceptives, and they work in all sorts of different ways. Some of them are shown below.

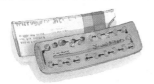

The pill is taken by women. It prevents ova maturing in the ovaries.

The cap needs to be smeared with a cream called 'spermicide'.

The sheath or condom is a thin rubber covering that fits onto a man's erect penis and stops sperm getting through.

The cap is a thin rubber dome that fits over a woman's cervix to stop sperm getting through.

Sexually transmitted diseases

During sexual intercourse, it is possible to pass on infections via the sex organs, known as venereal disease. Doctors can usually treat these successfully, though it is not yet possible to cure AIDS. These diseases are in most cases spread through unprotected sexual intercourse with someone with an unknown sexual history.

Growing a baby

Once the fertilized egg has sunk into the uterus wall, conception has taken place. At this stage, the woman will probably not realize that she is pregnant. She will find out when she misses her next period and gets the result of a pregnancy test.

Growing stages

It takes forty weeks for a baby to grow from a fertilized egg into a little human being, ready to be born.

During all that time, the baby relies on its mother's body completely. Its main growth stages are shown below.

Six weeks

The baby is about 2.4cm long. It hasn't developed much yet, and it looks a little bit like a tadpole, with stumpy buds instead of arms and legs. At this stage, the baby's heart begins to beat for the first time.

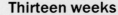

Thirteen weeks

The baby is now about 12cm long and weighs about 30g. It is developing more recognizably, and its legs, head, arms, face and internal organs are all perfectly formed by now.

At this stage, the baby starts to move around in the uterus, but not enough for the mother to feel.

Twenty-eight weeks

The baby is now about 30-36cm long and weighs about 900g. It is growing fast and there is more muscle on the body, but little fat. Its body is covered in a pale yellow wax called vernix, which protects the skin from the moisture of the fluid around it.

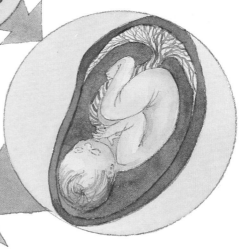

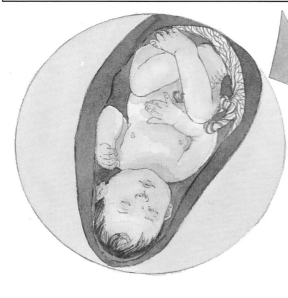

Forty weeks

The baby is approximately 50cm long and weighs about 3.4 kilos. It is now ready to be born. It has put on fat and looks chubby and rounded.

The mouth and eyelids lose their covering of vernix, so that they are ready to open as soon as the baby makes an entrance into the world outside!

Life in the womb

As the baby grows, the uterus grows and stretches to hold it.

The baby floats inside a fluid-filled bag called the amniotic sac.

The baby gets its food through the umbilical cord joined to its tummy. The cord is joined to the placenta, an organ which transfers food and oxygen to the baby from the mother's blood.

The baby's waste products are transferred back to the mother's blood via the umbilical cord and the placenta.

The baby needs to kick sometimes, to exercise its muscles. As the baby becomes stronger, the mother begins to feel the movement inside her stomach.

Waiting for a baby

Having a baby growing inside you can be a wonderful feeling. However, making a healthy baby is hard work for a woman's body. All through her pregnancy, she must get plenty of rest and food.

Every month or so, a pregnant woman will go to a hospital or a doctor for an ante-natal check-up (ante-natal means 'before birth').

Many women go to classes to learn how to give birth comfortably and prepare for what is going to happen. Babies' fathers can go to the classes, too.

Giving birth to a baby

Babies are expected to arrive after 40 weeks of pregnancy. Very few babies arrive exactly on the right date, but most are born within two weeks of it, either earlier or later.

1st stage — The start of labour

The first stage is the longest part of labour. The cervix opens and the uterus muscles begin to push the baby down. They pull the cervix up and open until it becomes a hole 10cm wide. These muscle movements are called contractions.

A woman knows she has started labour because she feels the contractions. The amniotic sac breaks and the sticky plug that shut the cervix during pregnancy comes out.

When the contractions begin to occur regularly every 5 minutes, it is time to call the midwife or go into hospital.

Giving birth can be hard work for the mother. The process is called being in labour, and can last from 2 to 36 hours. The labour usually goes through three different stages.

2nd stage — Giving birth

Once the cervix is wide open, the uterus muscles begin to push the baby out. The woman helps to push, too. She may want to kneel or squat to make the pushing easier to do.

The baby's head stretches the vagina, and if the vaginal opening looks too small, the midwife may make a small cut in it. Once the baby's head is out, the body follows quickly. It is then time to cut the umbilical chord.

3rd stage — The placenta

The last few contractions of the womb push out the placenta. It is important that all of it comes out because any pieces left in the uterus could cause infection.

If the baby is ill, or the mother cannot give birth to it normally, doctors perform a simple operation to open the uterus and lift the baby out. This is called a caesarean.

Labour pains

Special patterns of breathing, taught at ante-natal classes, can help to ease labour pain, together with pain-killing drugs. Some women want to have their babies without the help of drugs, using breathing alone.

What can dads do?

Many women have the baby's father or a friend or relative with them during labour. They can provide help and comfort during the birth.

Everybody's baby!

A baby's mother does the hard work of giving birth, but the whole family can help once the baby has been born and comes home.

Feeding the new-born baby

Every woman's breast contains cells that produce milk. They become active when a baby is born. Breast milk contains all the right ingredients a baby needs.

You can also feed a baby with manufactured 'formula' milk. However it has to be carefully prepared before use.

"I'll have to share my brother's room now."

"I wonder if babies can learn to play football?"

"They'll want me to babysit now."

"Ah well, sleepless nights again!"

"Ah well, back to the washing up. I wonder if anyone has fed the dog..."

"This must be home!"

"They've forgotten to feed me again. I'm leaving!"

Caring for your body

No-one enjoys being ill, and yet many people behave in a way that they know will make them ill or even kill them.

Smoking, drinking heavily or taking addictive drugs will ruin your mind and your body.

What is a drug?

A drug is a chemical that can change the way your mind and body work. Doctors sometimes prescribe medical drugs to help cure an illness, but there are other drugs which are more readily available. For instance, cigarettes contain a drug called nicotine, alcohol is a drug and the caffeine found in tea and coffee is a drug, too. All these substances will affect you in some way.

WARNING!
If you have taken strong drugs you don't think properly, so you are more prone to accidents.

WARNING!
Drugs tend to have unpleasant and damaging side effects on the body. These can be long-term.

WARNING!
Some drugs are addictive. The body comes to depend on them and craves for them.

Alcohol

Alcohol is a drug that changes the way you feel, even after small amounts. It affects your judgement and makes you slow to react. Many people are killed in road accidents every year because they drink and drive.

Long term damage to the body begins if you drink more than 4 pints of beer (or the equivalent in spirits) per day for a man, or 3 pints (or the equivalent) for a woman. This can lead to addiction and serious health problems, including liver and kidney failure, brain damage and stomach ulcers.

Cigarettes, cigars and pipes

Tobacco smoke contains nicotine plus 6,800 different chemicals. Several of these are known to cause cancer. Tobacco smoke stops the cleaning system of the lungs working, so that tar, chemicals and dirt accumulate in them. Smokers are prone to lung infections and chronic lung diseases such as bronchitis. They are also prone to heart disease.

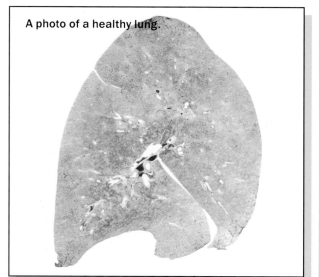

A photo of a healthy lung.

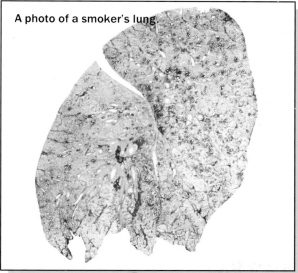

A photo of a smoker's lung.

It's never too late to stop!

It is difficult to give up smoking because nicotine is an addictive drug which the body craves for. The best thing is never to begin, but health starts to benefit the day a person gives up, no matter how long they have smoked.

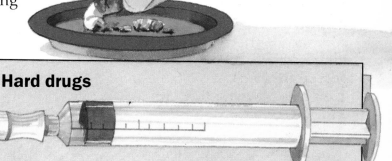

Hard drugs

Particularly addictive, dangerous substances are called 'hard drugs'. They include heroin and cocaine. Users get short term 'highs', but they suffer from mental and physical side effects which can kill them. Some addicts use surgical needles to inject drugs into themselves. If they share needles with other users, they may spread lethal diseases such as AIDS (see p. 39).

Body maintainance

Your body can take you anywhere and do almost anything you want it to! It has a built-in repair service and amazing powers of strength and stamina …. but ONLY if you take care of it! Here are some tips.

Your body surface provides a home for all sorts of bacteria and fungi. Most of the time these are harmless, but they can cause infection if they get out of control. If you wash thoroughly every day you will help to keep them in check.

Your body must get enough nutrients from the food you eat in order to work properly (see page 20). A good diet makes you feel energetic and alert and it also builds up your resistance to infections and diseases.

While you sleep, your body cleans away wastes and repairs damage, while your brain stores and processes all the information it has received during the day. So sleep is essential to health. The younger you are, the more sleep you need.

Eating a healthy diet and sleeping aren't enough to keep your body in really good condition. You need regular strenuous exercise, too, such as running, playing football, cycling, swimming or aerobics. It'll make you feel great!

What does exercise do?

Exercise builds stamina, makes your heart stronger and improves your circulation. It increases the amount of air your lungs can take in and it helps keep your weight down by increasing your energy output.

Exercise strengthens your muscles, making them bigger and more efficient. It stretches your joints, making them stronger and more supple. So fitness is the three S's: stamina, strength and suppleness! Improving your three S's will make you look and feel better.

Good exercises

Swimming and football are both good for building up the three S's. Alternatively, you could go for a combination of other exercises. Choose from options such as yoga, gymnastics, jogging, tennis and cycling.

Exercise stimulates the brain to make its own natural 'body drugs'. These substances create a feeling of well-being and happiness. So exercise can help get rid of depression and worry and give your brain a holiday!

How much exercise?

You don't have to be an Olympic athlete and spend hours exercising every day; but a gentle stroll to the bus stop isn't enough!

The minimum you should aim for is three 20-minute exercise sessions a week, during which your heart should beat faster and your breathing should get deeper.

It's up to you!

Some of the world's most common diseases are due to poor diet, smoking, drinking and lack of exercise. You can choose to smoke and drink, live on crisps and sweets and never take exercise … it's up to you. But remember, it's YOUR body, and it's up to YOU to look after it!

47

Index

Published by BBC Educational Publishing, a division of BBC Enterprises Limited, Woodlands, 80 Wood Lane, London W12 0TT.

First published 1990.

Devised and produced by Times Four Publishing Limited for BBC Enterprises Limited.

Paperback ISBN: 0 563 34602 7.
Hardback ISBN: 0 563 34755 4.

Printed in Great Britain by BPCC Paulton Books Ltd.

Typeset by TDR Photoset, Dartford, England.
Origination by RCS Graphics Ltd, Leeds, England.

Picture credits

cover Robin Wright/Tony Potter, **p3** Robin Wright/Tony Potter, **p13**, Science Photo Library, **p26** Robin Wright/Tony Potter, **p41** Robin Wright/Tony Potter, **p45** Science Photo Library, **p46** Robin Wright/Tony Potter, **p47** Robin Wright/Tony Potter.

With thanks to Terry Marsh, Executive Producer of Sex Education, and to Kerena Marchant, Programme Director.

Eyewitness
HUMAN BODY

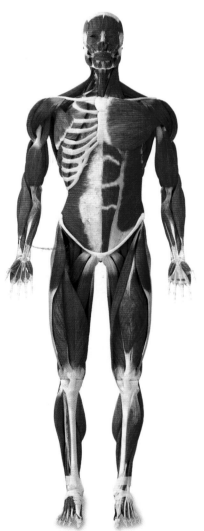

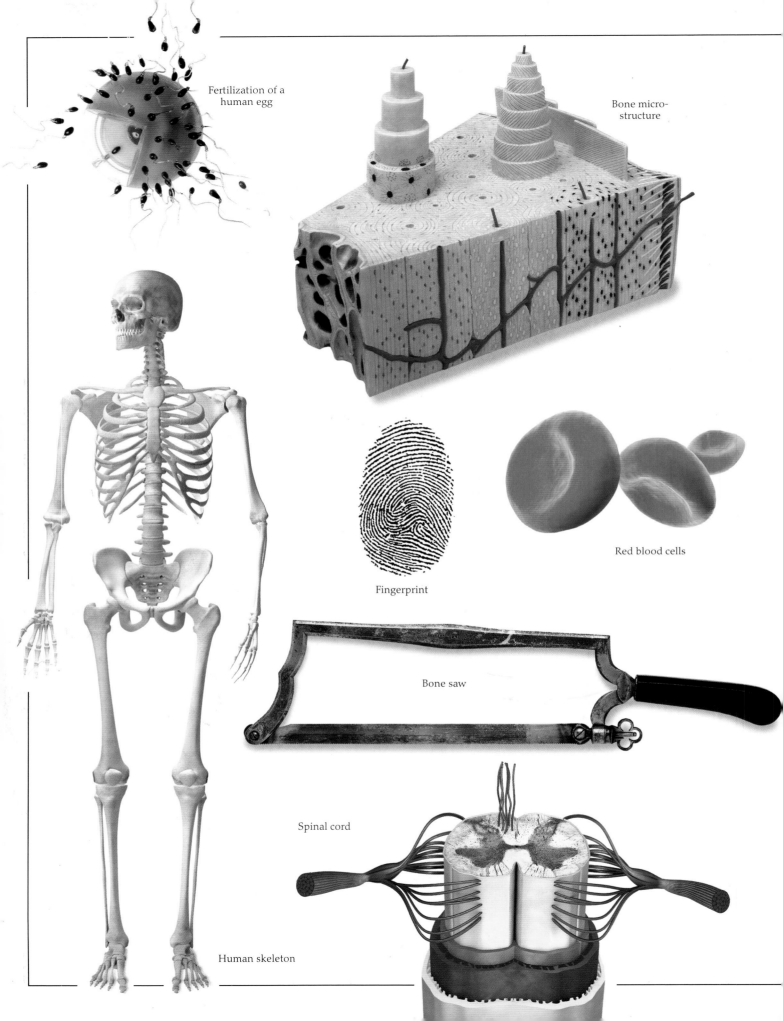

Fertilization of a human egg

Bone micro-structure

Fingerprint

Red blood cells

Bone saw

Spinal cord

Human skeleton